Tyrannosaurus Rex

Tyrannosaurus Rex

by Millicent Selsam

HARPER & ROW, PUBLISHERS
New York, Hagerstown, San Francisco, London

Photo credits:

Pages 4–5: Montana Department of Highways.

Pages 2, 6, 7, 9, 10–11, 12, 13, 14, 15, 16, 17, 18, 20 (Art by Charles R. Knight), 22, 23 (Art by Charles R. Knight), 25, 26, 28, 29, 31, 37: Courtesy of The American Museum of Natural History.

Page 30: Smithsonian Institution.

Pages 32–33, 34–35: Art by Charles R. Knight. Copyright Field Museum of Natural History, Chicago.

Library of Congress Cataloging in Publication Data
Selsam, Millicent Ellis, date
    Tyrannosaurus rex.

    SUMMARY: Describes efforts to reconstruct a
Tyrannosaurus rex skeleton from fossilized bones
found in Montana in 1901 and discusses resulting
deductions about the creature's way of life.
    1. Tyrannosaurus rex—Juvenile literature.
[1. Tyrannosaurus rex. 2. Dinosaurs]
I. Title.
QE862.D5S42 1978   568'.19   77–25677
ISBN 0–06–025423–8
ISBN 0–06–025424–6 lib. bdg.

To Laura

Tyrannosaurus Rex

AQUATIC DUCK-BILL DINOSAURS

Did you ever stand before the skeleton of a giant dinosaur and wonder where it was found, how it was found, and how it was put together?

This is the story of one of the fiercest dinosaurs that ever lived—how it was found, dug out of the rock, and mounted at a great museum.

Just after the turn of the century, a scientist from the New York zoo was out west hunting deer in a wild section of the state of Montana, near the Missouri River, when he found a pile of large bones. He took one home for a paperweight, and the friend who was with him took photographs of the bone pile and the area in which it was found.

In New York, the scientist showed the bone to Barnum Brown, a young assistant curator of fossil reptiles at The American Museum of Natural History. Barnum Brown was excited. The "paperweight" turned out to be the horn of a dinosaur, Triceratops. Other Triceratops bones had been found before, in a place in Wyoming where many other dinosaur fossils had been found.

3

Ever since the Civil War, dinosaur hunters had been scouring the states of Colorado, Montana, Wyoming, and Utah for dinosaur bones. Many had been found, but this new discovery in Montana was promising. Perhaps new kinds of dinosaurs would be found here!

The following year, 1902, an expedition of three scientists headed by Barnum Brown was sent to Montana near the Missouri River. The nearest railroad station was Miles City, 130 miles away. Every-

*Montana badlands in
Makoshika State Park*

thing had to be carried by horse and wagon, because this was before the day of automobiles. The expedition traveled for five days over prairies to a small town, Jordan, near Hell Creek. Just beyond Hell Creek the scene suddenly changes into badland—fantastic country where rivers and wind have cut through rocks so that there is practically no flat land, just canyons and cliffs of bright-colored rocks.

5

The expedition camped on Hell Creek near where the pile of bones had been discovered the year before. The hillside near them was mostly yellow sandstone, but harder big, bluish stones were scattered among the yellow rocks. The blue stones had tumbled down from the hillside to their camp. They contained bones!

Slowly, searching over every inch of ground, the

Tyrannosaurus quarry

Excavating with team of horses

scientists traced the stones up the side of the hill. Before the cook's call for dinner, they found some of the most interesting fossilized bones ever discovered.

They belonged to a dinosaur which later was named *Tyrannosaurus rex,* which means "king of tyrant lizards," because it was the biggest meat-eating animal ever to live on the earth.

The bones were lying where the dinosaur had fallen more than 70 million years ago. At that time the land was covered with marshes, lakes, forests, and plains. Tyrannosaurus might have died at the edge of a swamp and sunk into the sand at the bottom of the swamp. Over millions of years, layers of shifting sand covered its body and turned to stone. Tyrannosaurus' bones turned to stone too, because minerals from the water seeped through the hardening mud and sand and were deposited in the bones. Later the earth rose, and what was at the bottom of the swamp was raised up into a hill. There the bones of Tyrannosaurus lay until a river cut through and exposed the bones.

Once the bones were discovered, the scientists faced a big problem. How were they going to get these gigantic bones out of the rock? They needed more help, so they hired men to plow away the earth that covered the bones. But the sandstone was too hard to be plowed. The only way to get to the bones was to dynamite the sandstone. They blasted the stone away until they got down to within eight inches of the bone layer. Then they had to stop. It was unsafe to go any further. Now they had to use pickaxes, shovels, and big chisels. But as soon as bone was seen, the work with heavy

8

Blasting in Tyrannosaurus quarry

*Tyrannosaurus hipbone
and backbone in rock*

tools stopped. Then delicate instruments were used to loosen the stone around the bone.

The bones could not be taken out of the rocks all in one piece. They were too big for that, so the scientists had to cut the bones into pieces that could be taken out separately.

10

Although the bones had turned to stone, they
were delicate and could easily crack. If the work-
men tried to lift them up as they were, they would
fall to pieces. First they had to be covered with
shellac to hold them together. Then strips of burlap
dipped in plaster of Paris were wound around the

11

bones. After this, the bones were put into boxes packed with straw.

The largest block removed, containing the pelvis, or hipbone, weighed 4,150 pounds—over two tons! It took six horses to move it by sled to the main road, and four horses to pull it by wagon to the railroad.

Blue stone containing part of hipbone

Tyrannosaurus skull

Working on Tyrannosaurus skull

Stone containing fossilized bones being dragged out of quarry

It took two summers to get the rock containing the bones out of the hillside. It was hot, dirty work, with the temperature going up to 110°F at noon and no shade available.

Boxing Tyrannosaurus hipbones

Moving block containing fossil bones into laboratory

The bones traveled by railroad to The American Museum of Natural History in New York. When they reached the museum, all the wrapping had to be undone. The plaster jackets had to be stripped off, and the rock left around the bones had to be removed. This had to be done by specialists who knew how to tell the difference between the bone and the rock. Slowly but surely the bones were

16

chipped out of the rock with hammer and chisel. If one man worked around the clock without stopping, it would take a year or two to put together a small dinosaur. It took several years' work by a large staff just to get the bones of the huge Tyrannosaurus out of the rock.

When all the rock was cleared from the bones, the scientists at the museum found they had most of the skull and jaws, much of the backbone, ribs,

Working on Tyrannosaurus hipbones in block of rock

Neck vertebrae of Tyrannosaurus

hipbone, hind limbs, feet, and arm bone, but not the tail.

In 1908 Barnum Brown found another Tyrannosaurus skeleton in the same region in which the first one was found. This time there were a perfect skull and jaws, backbone, ribs, and hipbone, and nearly all of the tail, but no limbs. The two skeletons together provided practically all the bones needed to put this giant dinosaur together.

The next job was to put all the bones together just as they were in the living dinosaur. But nobody

18

had ever seen this animal before, so putting the bones together was like trying to put together the parts of a jigsaw puzzle without knowing what the picture is.

First they laid out the bones. Of course the head went at one end and the tail at the other. Then the rest of the bones had to be arranged in between. The scientists who worked on Tyrannosaurus knew bones very well. Besides, the bones of vertebrates—animals with backbones—are pretty similar. They all have backbones with vertebrae, and it is fairly easy to see how one vertebra fits into another. Vertebrates also have similar leg bones, arm bones, hipbones, and neck bones. Although the bones of Tyrannosaurus were huge, they did resemble other bones the scientists knew.

The mounting of the skeleton was most difficult. The size and weight of the bones was enormous. Some were so heavy that they had to be moved by a block and tackle that rode on an iron beam overhead. The bones had to be suspended from the beam to hold them in place until a steel framework could be built.

A steel rod was passed through the central canal of the spine to hold the vertebrae together. Small thin strips of steel had to be used to fix each rib in

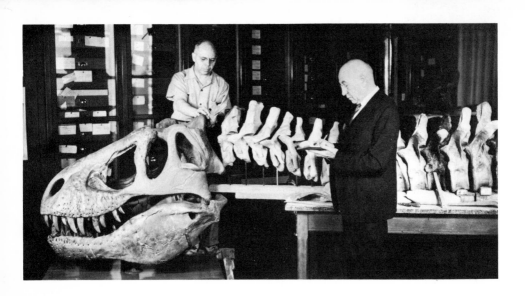

A Museum scientist and Dr. Barnum Brown working on the skeleton of Tyrannosaurus which went to the Carnegie Museum

place. Holes had to be drilled in bones that had no holes so that steel wire could be put through them. Big bones and little bones had to be strung together and supported by steel wires, bolts, screws and rods.

To help figure out the pose the skeleton should take, a small model of every bone in the skeleton was prepared, mounted, and studied.

Both of the skeletons found were mounted. If some bones were missing in one skeleton, plaster casts were made from the bones of the other skeleton and fitted in. Where a bone was missing from both specimens, a sculptor had to make a model of a bone by figuring out how it fitted into the bones nearest it.

If you ever see a Tyrannosaurus skeleton, you will be able to tell which parts are real bone and which were modeled because they are of a different color.

One of these skeletons was sold to the Carnegie Museum in Pittsburg in 1941, when The American Museum of Natural History was afraid that the only two skeletons of *Tyrannosaurus rex* in existence might be destroyed if New York was bombed by the Germans, with whom we were then at war.

The scientists who mounted the Tyrannosaurus skeleton at The American Museum of Natural History were amazed. Tyrannosaurus was about fifty feet long—longer than a city bus. It was twenty feet high—Tyrannosaurus was tall enough to stick its head into a second-story window. The knee joint alone was six feet above the ground—a tall man or woman standing next to Tyrannosaurus could just reach its knees. The head was five feet long—about as long as an average-size table. The teeth in its huge jaws were like daggers—each about six inches long.

An animal's teeth show whether it is a plant eater or a meat eater. If the teeth are pointed and

21

Tyrannosaurus skull

sharp, the animal surely feeds on the flesh of other animals. If most of an animal's teeth are flat grinding teeth like your back teeth, the animal is most likely a plant eater.

Tyrannosaurus' long sharp teeth showed that it was a meat eater, who probably fed on other dinosaurs. Its great mouth could open a yard wide to tear chunks of flesh.

Each hind foot spread out over more than seven square feet, and with one step it could cross a room. Its back legs were heavy and strong and were

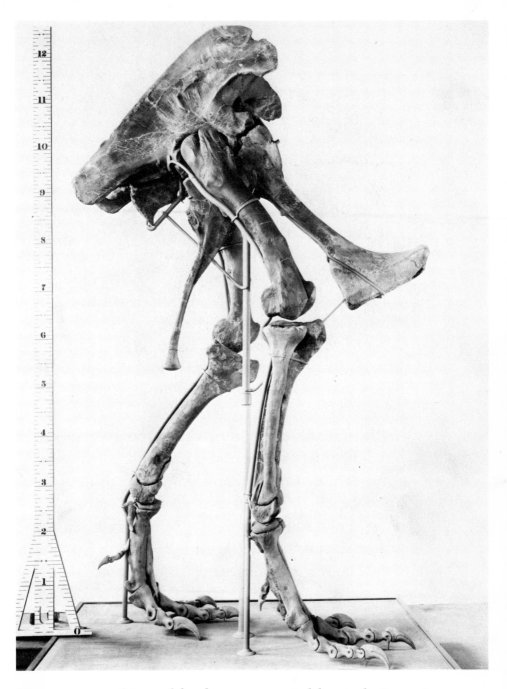

Tyrannosaurus hip and leg bones supported by steel pipes

equipped with enormous claws. The front limbs were stunted and small.

Since those two front limbs didn't reach the ground, scientists knew that Tyrannosaurus traveled on its two hind legs. It could not swim because it had no power in those puny front limbs. As a four-footed animal, it could not have lived in trees because it had no long front limbs for swinging from branch to branch and was too big and heavy to jump from branch to branch like a squirrel. They knew it didn't fly because there was no big breastbone to which wings could have been attached. So they concluded Tyrannosaurus had to walk on land on its two heavy, powerful hind legs.

Tyrannosaurus' fifty-foot body weighed about eight tons, almost as much as three average-sized elephants. It was balanced by a long, heavy tail.

From the skeleton it was possible to figure out just what Tyrannosaurus looked like with muscles and skin added. Bone is broadened or has a ridge where the big muscles are attached to it. And there is another clue: Bones are usually smooth, but they are scarred and pitted where smaller muscles are attached. When they had decided where all the muscles belonged and added flesh around the bones and muscles, the scientists at the museum were able to make a real model of Tyrannosaurus.

Mounting the Tyrannosaurus skeleton

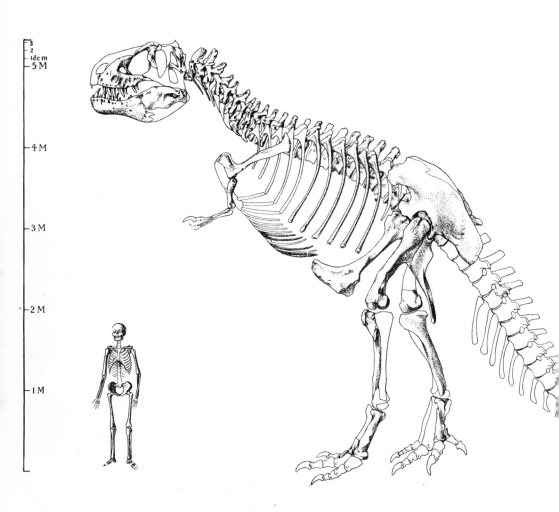

3
2
Idcm
5 M

4 M

3 M

2 M

1 M

When Tyrannosaurus lived, about 70 million years ago, there were multitudes of large, slow-moving, plant-eating dinosaurs that Tyrannosaurus could have fed on. Most of them were *duckbills*, which got their name from their broad, flat mouths, like the bills of ducks. They were generally tall, with long hind legs, shorter front legs, and heavy tails—a shape somewhat like a kangaroo. They could stand and walk on their two hind legs or drop down on all fours. Their heavy tails were flattened sideways like the tails of crocodiles and alligators, and their hands and feet were webbed like ducks' feet. For these reasons, scientists believed the duckbills to be swimmers.

The strangest thing about the duckbills was their heads. Although some were flat-headed, many had peculiar crests of bone on top of their heads. Inside the bones were twisted canals connected to the nostrils and windpipe. These canals may have given duckbills a good sense of smell.

Restored skeleton of Tyrannosaurus compared to a human skeleton

Duckbill dinosaurs

For a long time it was thought that duckbills used their peculiar mouths to shovel up food from the muddy bottoms of ponds. But new evidence shows that they used their grinding teeth (there were two thousand of them!) to crush twigs, leaves, and seeds of the evergreen and poplar trees along the shores of lakes and rivers.

Tyrannosaurus could easily have pounced on a duckbill and torn it apart. The duckbills had only a few defenses. They could smell danger if Tyrannosaurus was near. Or they could use their keen eyesight to check the landscape for their chief enemy. So if they had time, they could jump into the water and swim away.

Tyrannosaurus probably also preyed on the many horned and armored dinosaurs that lived at the same time. One of the common horned dinosaurs was Triceratops. It was about twenty-five feet

Skull of Triceratops in quarry

long—about as long as one and a half average automobiles. It had an enormous head with a great bony collar at the back of it. A huge horn came out above each eye, and a shorter horn emerged from its nose. These three horns gave Triceratops its name, which means "three horns on the face." Triceratops could stuff lots of plants into its huge mouth. Tyrannosaurus went after Triceratops, but probably did not always win the battle, for Triceratops could have defended itself and rammed Tyrannosaurus with its three horns.

Triceratops skeleton restored

Triceratops

Another common armored dinosaur that Tyrannosaurus fed on was Ankylosaurus. It had bony plates all over its body and a tail with projecting bony spikes that could lash around and inflict terrible wounds. If it was attacked by Tyrannosaurus, Ankylosaurus could curl up like an armadillo.

Triceratops and Ankylosaurus were only two of the many horned and armored dinosaurs alive at the same time as Tyrannosaurus.

31

An armored dinosaur called Paleoscincus

The duckbills could escape from Tyrannosaurus by swimming away, having been warned by their keen senses of smell and sight. The armored and horned dinosaurs could protect themselves by their armor and horns. But other, smaller, dinosaurs had other ways of escaping Tyrannosaurus. Struthiomimus, for example, who looked something like an ostrich without feathers but with a

A duckbill dinosaur called Edmontosaurus

long tail, could run away on feet like a bird's. It was probably much faster moving than Tyrannosaurus.

Yet in spite of all these ways other dinosaurs had of protecting themselves from Tyrannosaurus, we know that Tyrannosaurus must often have caught or won battles with them. Otherwise, Tyrannosaurus would not have survived for long.

33

It may seem that we now know all there is to know about Tyrannosaurus, but this is far from the truth. There are still many mysteries to clear up.

Scientists are now considering whether Tyrannosaurus and other dinosaurs might have been warm-blooded, rather than the cold-blooded reptiles we have always thought them to be. They reason that it must have taken great energy for Tyrannosaurus to move its enormous body in search for food, and the creature would have

Triceratops

needed warm-bloodedness to produce this energy. Perhaps it was not a clumsy, slow-moving giant but a swift-moving killer?

Tyrannosaurus' front legs have always been something of a mystery. What good were these puny legs that could not even reach Tyrannosaurus' mouth? Actually, some scientists think that they may have reached the mouth. Each forelimb had two sharp claws curved like an eagle's. Could they have been used like hooks to hold prey?

Tyrannosaurus

Or were these forelimbs no use at all in feeding? Might they have been used as props to help raise Tyrannosaurus off the ground to a standing position?

Many books show one Tyrannosaurus fighting with another over the body of the prey. But we really do not know whether this actually happened. Perhaps each Tyrannosaurus had its own territory and did not fight with its neighbors over prey. Perhaps they just fought over the boundaries of their territory and then left each other alone.

We still do not know what color Tyrannosaurus was. Was it red like a coral snake? Was it green like the green turtle? Was it striped? We will probably never find out.

There are many theories about why Tyrannosaurus and all the other dinosaurs died out suddenly about 70 million years ago. Some scientists have suggested that a giant star (supernova) exploded near the earth and exposed the earth to radiation equal to billions of tons of hydrogen bombs.

We know that great mountain ranges were built up at this time. Did the swamps and lakes where dinosaurs lived suddenly disappear?

36

Tyrannosaurus skeleton

Different kinds of vegetation such as flowering plants and new kinds of trees appeared at this time too. Were the dinosaurs unable to feed on these new types of plants?

We still do not have all the answers.

BIBLIOGRAPHY

Augusta, J. *Prehistoric Animals.* Spring Books, 1956.

Brown, Barnum. Field Notes in Archives of The American Museum of Natural History, 1902–1905.

Colbert, Edwin. *The Dinosaur Book.* New York: McGraw-Hill, Inc., 1951.

_____. *Dinosaurs, Their Discovery and Their World.* New York: E. P. Dutton & Co., Inc., 1964.

_____. *Evolution of the Vertebrates.* New York: John Wiley & Sons, Inc., 1969.

_____. *Men and Dinosaurs.* New York: M. Evans & Co., Inc., 1969.

Desmond, A. J. *The Hot-Blooded Dinosaurs.* New York: The Dial Press, 1976.

Fox, W., and Welles, S. *From Bones to Bodies.* New York: Henry Z. Walck, 1959.

Glut, Donald F. *Dinosaur Dictionary.* Secaucus, N. J.: Citadel Press, 1972.

Lanham, U. N. *Bone Hunters.* New York: Columbia University Press, 1973.

Ostrom, Dr. John H. *The Strange World of the Dinosaurs.* New York: G. P. Putnam's Sons, 1964.

Owen, Ellis. *Prehistoric Animals.* London: Octopus Books, Ltd., 1975.

Simpson, G. G. *Life of the Past.* New Haven: Yale University Press, 1953.

Sternberg, C. H. *The Life of a Fossil Hunter*. New York: Henry Holt & Co., 1909.

Swinton, W. E. *The Dinosaurs*. New York: John Wiley & Sons, Inc., 1970.

Time-Life Editors. *The Emergence of Man*. New York: Time-Life Books, 1972.

Watson, Jane W. *Giant Golden Book of Dinosaurs and other Prehistoric Reptiles*. New York: Golden Press, Inc., 1960.

Whitaker, G. *Dinosaur Hunt*. New York: Harcourt, Brace and World, Inc., 1965.

INDEX